Dedicated to William

Healing is the direct result from living life through the three L's:
love, laws, and light.

The purpose of this dictionary is to assist in understanding all your heavy emotions and transmute them into emotions from the light. In this time of confusion, contradiction and concern, it is extremely important that we learn self knowledge, self awareness and self transformation.

We co-created the problems and now let us co-create the solutions. We have, as a society, emotionally branded ourselves with shame. There is the angry man, the depressed woman, the abusive parent, the out of control child; all these being interchangeable with each other. Healing begins with self respect, enabling us to give more respect to others, whether that be a person, an animal or the planet. In turn, we create a more loving atmosphere for ourselves and all those surrounding us.

Anything that divides us from love needs to be abolished. Anything that separates us from bliss needs to be re-created. Let us use our mistakes as learning experiences, not allowing them to cause permanent damage to our souls. We need to look at our shortcomings with sharper awareness and softer eyes. In turn, we respond to life intelligently instead of reacting irrationally.

Peace of mind must first be adopted within ourselves before we are equipped to handle things outside ourselves. The more we develop skills of integrity (love), intelligence (laws), and inspiration (light), the more we discover our full potential and empowerment.

We enter and leave this world with only our souls, therefore, we must learn to live THROUGH our souls. What is a soul? Quite simply, it is connected to our heart. It speaks to us through our heartfelt feelings. Hidden in those feelings are our highest truths.

When our heavy emotions control our lives, we are slaves. When our good thoughts control our lives, we are students. When light and love control our lives, we are Masters. Our Divine spark is re-ignited and we re-claim our authenticity and electricity. Only then do we realize that we are, indeed, the heroes and heroines we have been searching for.

1

Table of Contents

Feelings	Page
Abandoned - Cherished	5
Abused - Nurtured	6
Ambivalent - Committed	7
Angry - Serene	8
Apathetic - Passionate	9
Argumentative - Harmonious	10
Arrogant - Humble	11
Ashamed - Proud	12
Asleep - Awakened	13
Betrayed - Loyal	14
Bitter - Sweet	15
Bored - Inspired	16
Brokenhearted - Blissful	17
Burdened - Uplifted	18
Careless - Careful	19
Cautious - Daring	20
Cheapened - Precious	21
Close-minded - Open-minded	22
Confused - Clear	23
Controlling - Allowing	24
Corrupt - Pure	25
Cowardly - Courageous	26
Cruel - Kind	27
Darkened - Enlightened	28
Deceptive - Honest	29
Defeated - Triumphant	30
Depressed - Excited	31
Destructive - Creative	32
Devastated - Ecstatic	33
Disappointed - Delighted	34
Discouraged - Encouraged	35
Doubting - Trusting	36
Egotistical - Spiritual	37
Exhausted - Energetic	38
Fearful - Safe	39
Frustrated - Fulfilled	40
Greedy - Sharing	41
Grieving - Joyful	42

Table of Contents

ABANDONED – heavy emotion

Abandoned: *given up, forsaken, deserted, responsibilities not lived up to.*

Abandonment is a means of madness. It breaks the heart and sears the soul. It is up to each and every one of us to take the steps to put an end to it, whether it be in our own life or in the life of another. The vast majority of our population has been abandoned in some way or another. It could have been by a teacher, a co-worker, a parent, the government, our children or, the worst….ourselves. It is such an everyday occurrence, that sometimes we do not even know it is happening. Be conscious, be concerned, be committed to constructive, caring communication. Indeed, it will be worth it….because it will make life more worthwhile.

Remember: If we do not handle our wounds, we abandon our wellness. If we do not handle our shame, we abandon our sacredness.

⌇ TRANSFORMATION ⌇

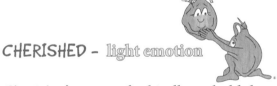

CHERISHED – light emotion

Cherished: *to care for kindly, to hold dear, to treat with tenderness.*

Cherishing others is a means of enrichment that knows no boundaries. It is living in a constant state of being in love. To be in love is to be enlivened. When we cherish another, we automatically start to cherish ourselves. On the other hand, when we cherish ourselves, we automatically start to cherish others. It creates a weather map in our lives of wellness, wealth and wonder. Our desires then become our realities and our dreams become our daily lives.

ABUSED – heavy emotion

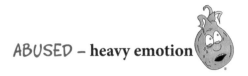

Abused: *hurt by being treated badly; insulted by coarse language, mistreated.*

Abuse is our planet's biggest problem, where global insanity reigns. World peace will begin if each and every one of us takes responsibility for not abusing another and not allowing ourselves to be abused. People who abuse others, more often than not, have been abused themselves. It is learned behavior. However, abusiveness leaves soul scars, whether one is abused or the abuser. People who have been exposed to abusiveness tend to see the glass as half empty instead of half full. They focus on their pain instead of on their pleasure. It is a wound that needs daily care. Where there is hatred, create honor; where there is cruelty, create kindness; where there is violence, create vigilance; where there is victim hood, create victory.

Remember: If we have been abused, it is no excuse to abuse another. If we abuse another, we are really abusing ourselves.

⤳ TRANSFORMATION ⤳

NURTURED – light emotion

Nurtured: *fed, supported, protected, encouraged.*

Nurturing is love put to practical use. Being nurtured or nurturing another, repairs a multitude of wounds, thus creating a world of wellness. It has been and always will be in our nature to nurture. It is why we were given a heart. Staying in tune with that part of ourselves creates a melodic rhythm that is music for our souls. It orchestrates an awareness of an angelic presence that wants to guide us to our greatness.

AMBIVALENT – **heavy emotion**

Ambivalent: *experiencing conflicting feelings; having contradictory and opposing emotions at the same time.*

Ambivalence is the main reason that marriages fail, businesses fail, children go awry and dreams die. Working with a divided mind almost always gives results that are less than hoped for. Nothing can work without commitment. Most of us want a guarantee first, and then decide if we want to commit, but by that point, it is already too late. If there is anything we want or anyone we want to be with, we need to be committed to making it happen. No matter what the outcome, the gift is ours because we will know that we did everything we could to make it possible. As Margaret Mead once said "Never doubt that a small group of thoughtful, committed citizens can change the whole world – indeed it is the only thing that ever will!"

Remember: To know commitment is to know contentment.

⌒ TRANSFORMATION ⌒

COMMITTED – light emotion

Committed: *given in trust, to pledge to, to entrust, to devote.*

Definite-ism is stronger than optimism, making life so simple because it eradicates all fear of not having love or success. What yeast is to bread, commitment is to life….we cannot rise without it. Commitment funds a confidence that needs no explanation. We are prepared to win, yet if we cannot, we are brave in the attempt. To be committed is to live each day as if it were our last!

ANGRY – heavy emotion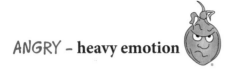

Angry: *stormy, inflamed, sore.*

Anger is the most confusing emotion. Half the population believes they could not survive without it, therefore relying on it and half the population believes they are terrible for having it, therefore denying it. Edgar Cayce said it best, "For those who are not angry are worth little – for those who lose their temper are worth less." Anger is a reaction, not an action. It is a reaction to fear, helplessness, frustration, or abandonment. Usually, we store anger, instead of addressing it, and then project it onto others. Anger, when utilized properly, can be our greatest motivator and achiever. Righteous anger activates us to want to change something and make a difference. The "reaching the bottom" anger activates us to change ourselves and make ourselves different. We need to study our anger to understand the root of our anger. We need to be certain it is our own and not someone else's. We will then be able to use it to propel ourselves into a greater state of being and awareness.

Remember: Conquering our anger with love will insure our triumph with no after-sorrow.

⤳ TRANSFORMATION ⤳

SERENE – light emotion

Serene: *peaceful, tranquil, clear, fair.*

Serenity is a state of mind that comes from detachment, discernment and devotion. We become gifted in the ways of infusing simple truths into complexities. We are corded to our own divine nature, whereby we do not fall into the confused conditioning of this world. To feel serene is the result of us quelling our inferior emotions and mastering our superior mindfulness. This, in itself, creates a sense of willingness and wellness for ourselves and all those surrounding us.

APATHETIC – heavy emotion

Apathetic: *lack of interest, lack of emotion, listless, indifferent.*

If we don't stand for something, we stand for nothing. Most people believe that the problems are too big and they are too small to make any difference. This is the root of apathy. It is true that we cannot change all situations. We certainly cannot change another person, but what we can do is change ourselves. We can no longer afford indifference. If everyone would put an intention on helping someone or something each day, we would eliminate hunger, spiritual poverty and war. A one hundred foot redwood tree starts with but a tiny seed. Know that we can be that seed. Sometimes, when we consider what tremendous successes come from little things, we realize that, in fact, there are no little things.

Remember: We must not let others invade our sense of purpose.

ᴄᴏ TRANSFORMATION ᴏᴄ

PASSIONATE – light emotion

Passionate: *enthusiastic, strong compelling feeling.*

Passion is the horsepower for our soul's desires. It is the instigator of opportunities that make us excited, igniting us to walk through the fires. To feel passionate is to feel excited, exhilarated and exonerated. It is the illumination of our imagination, lighting the path to our destiny. Life without passion is a life without purpose. Life with passion is a life potent with our potential.

ARGUMENTATIVE – **heavy emotion**

Argumentative: *controversial, contentious, disagreeing.*

There is a great difference between arguing and being argumentative. To argue is to give reasons for and against something that we believe in. It is a platform for our opinions. Being argumentative is staged for overriding someone else's opinion. It is important to stand up for ourselves without pushing someone else down. Let our intentions for our arguments always come from a pure and loving space. Masters teach these three steps: look a person in the eye, own our own opinion and then be clear. This lays the foundation for true communication and leaves no space for making someone else wrong.

Remember: When stating a point of view; be conscious – not contentious; be kind, not cutting; be concerned, not condemning.

∽ TRANSFORMATION ∽

HARMONIOUS – light emotion

Harmonious: *marked in agreement of feeling, consistently pleasing, free from discord.*

When our hands and our heart walk in balance with one another, we create a feeling of wellness that can only be described as heavenly. It is our mastery in the making. Harmony is the collaboration of empathy and equality between ourselves and another, leaving no room for adversity. It is the grace of patient acceptance and the ability to conform to all conditions peacefully.

ARROGANT - **heavy emotion**

Arrogant: *filled with unwarranted pride and self importance.*

Arrogance is birthed from low self-esteem. For those of us who know more than others, for those of us who do better than others, for those of us who are more spiritually aware than others, for those of us who have more than others, for those of us who are more athletically inclined than others.... know this! It is our responsibility to take others by the hand and show them the way with love, compassion and humility. It is our responsibility to give thanks every day for gifts that we have that others do not. One who embraces humbleness is rarely humiliated. It is that simple.

Remember: People who are humble know that an apology is a great way of having the last word!

⤳ TRANSFORMATION ⤳

HUMBLE - light emotion

Humble: *respectful, without false pride, unassuming.*

To be humble is to be honorable. It is the sign that nothing has to happen outside of ourselves for us to feel worthy and wonderful. Humbleness is a recognition that our abilities come from a power much greater than ourselves. This leads to a knowingness of who we are, what we want and where we want to be in our life. We have nothing to prove to anyone, except ourselves, masters of our own fate. Being humble creates a harmonic convergence of sensitivity, safety and serenity.

ASHAMED – heavy emotion

Ashamed: *humiliated, embarrassed, sense of inadequacy or inferiority.*

Shame disconnects us from our Divine potential. It is the poison that has been passed down from generation to generation. Battles were won on shaming others. If we are ever to see peace on earth, we must eliminate actions that cause this emotion. The only way this can occur is to be in charge of our own behavior. No matter how upset we are, let us not do anything to shame ourselves. We need to be our own best friend and own best partner. We must never be led into a state of selfishness or meanness, for in the end, we will be riddled with shame. Following the 4 G's: goodness, generosity, genuineness and grace will be the refinement of our reasoning and the alignment of our actions.

Remember: We must not sell ourselves *short*. Instead let us hold ourselves responsible for a *taller* standard than anyone expects of us.

↩ TRANSFORMATION ↪

PROUD – light emotion

Proud: *highly honorable or creditable , satisfied self-esteem*

There is a fine line between proud and prideful. Prideful is being haughty and arrogant. Proud comes from making decisions that are self respecting. They generate an energy of honor and reverence. We can never go wrong if we live life in the truest sense of the word proud:

Purity-Reverence-Openheartedness-Understanding-Discipline.

ASLEEP – heavy emotion

Asleep: *numb, inactive, sluggish, dull.*

As a society, we are sleep walkers. By and large, we are so busy making a living, we do not take the time to make a life. Most people give up because they do not believe that they can have what they want. Do not buy into this – do not give in – fight back! Our soul is waiting in the wings, wanting to fly. We need to know that we can have whatever we want – maybe not today, maybe not tomorrow, but if we keep our intention on it, it will indeed manifest. Keep energized, stay alive. When we are out of touch with ourselves, we cannot touch another. We cannot be the difference we promised ourselves. Let us not fall asleep at the wheel; instead let us drive ourselves to be what we dreamed of and have all we planned for.

Remember: Unveil the higher aspects, unleash the hidden power.

☙ TRANSFORMATION ❧

AWAKENED – light emotion

Awakened: *active, alert, vigilant, alive.*

Miracles do happen, we just have to stay up to be part of them. To be awakened is to be aligned with the highest good for ourselves and others. It facilitates a consciousness that keeps our eyes wide open. We begin to see things we never thought possible, we begin to hear things we never dreamt probable. Being awakened creates a portal of wondrous things happening beyond our wildest imagination. It is the vital force that attends transformation.

BETRAYED – **heavy emotion**

Betrayed: *deceived, to break faith with, to be seduced and then deserted.*

Ever since the beginning of time, betrayal is what has befallen most of the world's important leaders. Unbeknownst to ourselves, we can walk into this energy at any time and find ourselves being betrayed or betraying another. Either way, it is excruciating to the heart. It diminishes all in whom it takes possession. We must return to honor and honesty. We need to become people of our word and subsequently hold others accountable for theirs. It has been noted that betrayal after trust is deadly to the soul. Creating heartfelt, truthful communication wherever we can becomes our life line. Forgiveness should not be far behind – it is the period at the end of the sentencing.

Remember: Betrayal to oneself is the worst betrayal of all.

↩ TRANSFORMATION ↩

LOYAL – light emotion

Loyal: *faithful to one's allegiance, oaths and obligations.*

Loyalty is what all good relationships must be built upon. Love without loyalty is like a garden without water. Nothing beautiful can really grow from it. Loyalty is the fundamental foundation of all that is fruitful. It creates a space between people, whereby our souls do not become tested but instead become rested. Serenity will come with loyalty, as loyalty will come with serenity.

BITTER – heavy emotion

Bitter: *harsh, severe, piercing.*

There is not one person in this world who cannot find something to be bitter about. In the word bitter is the word bite. People who are bitter usually have a "biting tongue" or they "bite the hand that feeds them". Biting is a cutting way of fighting! It would be to the betterment of our life's journey to know that no one else can em-bitter us. We must make a commitment to our own sweet nature. It is our insurance policy for our happiness. Changing our authentic nature pierces our innocence and vitality. It hardens the heart and stings the soul.

Remember: Bitterness taxes us, whereas sweetness relaxes us.

⤸ TRANSFORMATION ⤸

SWEET – light emotion

Sweet: *pleasing, agreeable in disposition*

Hummingbirds are known as the happiness birds. They live and thrive on sweet syrup. There is a belief that if a hummingbird is unhappy, it dies. The same goes for our souls. Therefore, we have a responsibility to our own personal path. Sweetness is our soul singing. Whenever we are sweet to someone, more often than not, light is not far behind. Whenever someone is sweet to us, more often than not love is not far behind.

BORED – heavy emotion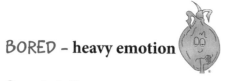

Bored: *dull, uninteresting, weary, monotonous.*

Many times, when children feel depressed, they express it by saying they are bored. Similarly, when adults feel hopeless, they express it by saying they are bored. Boredom comes from despair. It is a statement of, "What's the use? Why bother? Who cares anyway?" The negativity that is fed to us each day certainly does not help. The news media, films and television programs strip us of our vibrancy, our vitality and our vigor. Therefore, we need to shift the focus to ourselves and our own life. We ALL have gifts and it is our responsibility to bring those unique gifts to the world. It is of the utmost importance that we source our purpose for being here. We are privileged souls, lucky to be in the world at such an opportune time in history. It has been said that if we are bold, not bored, mighty forces will come to our aid.

Remember: Be an eagle that is soaring, not a human that is boring.

↩ TRANSFORMATION ↪

INSPIRED – light emotion

Inspired: *to arouse, to generate, to fill with an exalted influence, to guide with divine influence.*

To feel inspired is our passion meeting our purpose. It ignites our spark and infuses us with hope and happiness. Our inspiration is our invitation to our universal connection. It is the awakening of the divine genes that live within us. Inspiration is a direct passage that bypasses the mind and kindles our creativity. When inspired....we never feel tired!

BROKENHEARTED – heavy emotion

Brokenhearted: *crushed by sorrow, grief, inconsolable.*

It is claimed that every tear holds one thousand emotions. It releases all the toxins and poisons from our system. Yet, we live in a world that perceives weeping as a weakness, not a strength. The first thing a doctor does when a baby is born is to encourage him or her to cry. To weep is to breathe – to breathe is to live. Crying relaxes the mind, cleanses the body, reforms the emotions and repairs the soul. Many times our lessons from feeling brokenhearted teach us how to be more openhearted. It deepens our connection to our own depth.

Remember: CRY is Consciousness Reaching You!

⤳ TRANSFORMATION ⤳

BLISSFUL – light emotion

Blissful: *supreme happiness, heaven, paradise.*

Bliss is the knowing that there is an exquisite place within us that no one and nothing can destroy. It is an experience of heaven manifesting on earth. Feeling blissful is a blessing in itself. Before it can happen, we must expect it to happen. It takes intention and attention. Affirming it is possible, makes it probable. Bliss comes from the disconnection between what our logical mind thinks of us and what the magnificent Universe knows of us. It reveals the illumination of our destiny.

BURDENED – heavy emotion

Burdened: *carrying a heavy load, feeling weighed down, hard to bear.*

Feeling burdened is an illusion. It is all a state of mind. If truth be known, we are only living one percent of our potential. Statistics show, we live in a world where 20% of the people are doing 80% of the work. The time has come for us to welcome responsibility. It is what keeps the brain blooming and the soul soaring. To be responsible is to be spiritually vibrant. We were given burdens, but we were also given shoulders. Mother Teresa is a perfect example; a 90 pound woman who was able to move mountains. When asking the question, "Why doesn't somebody do something?", wake up….we are that somebody!

Remember: No involvement, no evolvement.

ᔐ TRANSFORMATION ᔐ

UPLIFTED – light emotion

Uplifted: *to raise up, to improve intellectually, emotionally or morally.*

Law of the Universe: when lifting up another, we always get lifted. It is the agreement from the Heavens. Nothing will make us happier than serving a cause greater than ourselves. Our bodies become rejuvenated and our spirits become revitalized. It is serving with the higher elements and reigning over the lower elements. To uplift is to uphold all that is upright.

CARELESS – **heavy emotion**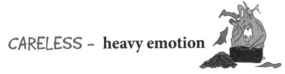

Careless: *done without enough attention, not thorough, unstudied, neglected.*

Many tragedies are caused by carelessness. This can be from the extreme of an accident to the everyday occurrence of a bounced check or a bill not paid on time. We live amidst a very impatient society. People want what they want when they want it. We are always in a hurry and most time, to go nowhere. This is a battle that must be won; we need to take it back and make it right. When rushing or agitated, take the time to stop…. breathe….think….then continue. Masters teach four steps to live wisely: learn broadly, examine completely, discern clearly and practice exactly.

Remember: When we take the time to inspect something; we are taking the time to respect something….and it is usually ourselves.

∾ TRANSFORMATION ∾

CAREFUL – light emotion

Careful: *done with accuracy, done with caution.*

There are so many options and choices in this world; we must be smart in what we stand for and careful in what we fall for. Watch for red flags, be willing to listen and be wise. It is important to trust our feelings because they let us know when something is out of place. To be careful is to be full of care. "Do not be fooled" is the same as "do not be foolish!"

CAUTIOUS – heavy emotion

Cautious: *too careful, too guarded, being on guard, wary.*

On the one hand, caution is important; yet on the other, being too cautious stops the flow of our natural life force. It is important to discern between the two. Being too cautious stops our ability to catch up with our enthusiasm. The person who does nothing but wait for their ship to come in has already missed the boat. Take the risk; the brave may not live forever, but the overly cautious do not live at all. Dive in to life, heaven has a history of using the insignificant to accomplish the impossible. Be realistic – plan a miracle.

Remember: Being wary makes us weary.

⤶ TRANSFORMATION ⤶

DARING – light emotion

Daring: *adventurous, courageous, heroic, bold.*

People who achieve mastery dare to do what they know to be right for themselves in the face of all obstacles and adversity. Being daring comes from a willingness to explore without any logical explanation. It is the ability to feel the enthusiasm of what could be and the acceptance of what might not be. Dare to be the difference that makes the difference.

CHEAPENED – heavy emotion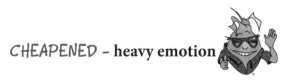

Cheapened: *belittled, depreciated, brought into contempt.*

We tend to treat each other with such disrespect. Every religion believes they have the right answer more than another; every sacred tribe has been diminished to nothing; men and women are at odds with each other and animals are treated as if they have no soul. In the midst of this destruction, how can we maintain our connection to our Divinity? It is time for a new world, a world built on spiritual healing. It is the moment when elections are won on merit, not misery; when men and women get along because they have mutual respect; where religions bow to each other because of their uniqueness; where tribes are honored because of their sacredness; and where we learn to love ourselves for the diamonds that we really are.

Remember: Do not measure – just treasure.

⤳ TRANSFORMATION ⤳

PRECIOUS – light emotion

Precious: *great value, highly loved, beautifully refined.*

When we are born, we are like precious jewels being brought into the world. Unfortunately, as times goes on and life happens as it does, we lose that feeling of worthiness. Treating ourselves and others preciously transcends the physical world and transcends the forces of dishonor. However, it takes a commitment to be constantly conscious, consistently concerned and continually connected.

CLOSE-MINDED - heavy emotion

Close-minded: *not receptive to new or different ideas, not open to further analysis, exclusive, limited.*

To be close-minded is to be unteachable. To be closed is to be out of touch with ourselves. To be out of touch with ourselves is to be out of touch with others. The root of being closed is fear – fear of something different than we are used to. Never be afraid of change. Change happens whether we are comfortable with it or not. The real voyage of discovery consists not in seeking new landscapes but in having new eyes. Let us get ready to sacrifice what we are for what we can become. The journey of a thousand miles begins with one step.

Remember: Nothing can come through a closed door; likewise, nothing can be given to those who keep their arms crossed.

⤳ TRANSFORMATION ⤳

OPEN-MINDED - light emotion

Open-minded: *having a mind receptive to new ideas, unprejudiced, impartial.*

To be open is to be one with the Universe and its unlimited potential. The mind is like a parachute, it only works when open. To be open to grow, one must be open to greet. What lies ahead of us is much more delightful than that which lies behind us. Everything exciting and exquisite comes from our willingness to expand. We must live each day as if it were our last.

CONFUSED – heavy emotion

Confused: *mixed up, bewildered, jumbled.*

Confusion defeats our empowerment. It leaves us paralyzed and helpless. We live in a world with so many options and opinions. We have forgotten how to keep things simple. When an event happens, we have dozens of news stations giving us thousands of versions of what REALLY happened. What is the truth? These times call for us to listen to our inner knowing and infinite intelligence. We need to quiet and center ourselves. We will then hear the whisperings of our wings and wisdom. We are all endowed with a clarity of truth that is just momentarily lost and waiting to be found.

Remember: Victory is lost through confusion and vacillation and won through clarity and certainty.

⤳ TRANSFORMATION ⤳

CLEAR – light emotion

Clear: *free from cloudiness, easily seen, sharply defined, easily understood, free from obstructions.*

When we are clear about something, we are at peace. When we use our ears to hear what is really being said and our eyes to see what is beneath the surface, then there will be no illusions or delusions. Peace of mind comes from presence of mind. It is a commitment to our own authenticity. Crystal clear clarity is knowing where we have been, where we are presently and where we are going. It is the pathway to our priorities and our purpose.

CONTROLLING – heavy emotion

Controlling: *to curb, to restrain, to regulate.*

The people who usually want to control are those who feel the most out of control. There is much time spent on people trying to change each other, when, in fact, we need only want to change ourselves. When we realize that nothing outside of ourselves can give us peace, it is then that we become at peace. We become unattached and find solace in our own life's journey. We develop an understanding that we are all different, which becomes an open forum for newness within ourselves.

Remember: To control does not leave much room for the soul to reach its predestined goal.

⟿ TRANSFORMATION ⟿

ALLOWING – light emotion

Allowing: *to permit, to acknowledge, to concede, to make provisions.*

People who do not concern themselves with loss or gain are people who do not need to be concerned. They are free to be authentically themselves and allow others be themselves. They have a wisdom of acceptance that goes beyond worldly attachments. They know that our path is not to see through one another but to see one another through. To be allowing is to be enlightened.

CORRUPT - **heavy emotion**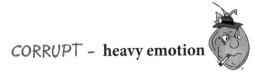

Corrupt: *contaminated, deteriorated, morally unsound.*

Unfortunately, corruption is flowing through the mainstream of our society. It stems from being attached to getting something for ourselves at all costs, no matter what the consequences are for another. It is linked to the demands of our times and is the result of deviating from one's spiritual origin. When one uses the mind in wrong relationship to the truth, certain destructive processes set in and thus corruption begins. It is a time when truth and sincerity are pivotal. Do not be fooled; the virtue of one individual is a secret measure by which a whole nation can improve.

Remember: Sometimes just one PURE interruption can stop a multitude of corruption.

∽ TRANSFORMATION ∽

PURE - light emotion

Pure: *clear, spotless, untainted, free from moral defilement.*

Purity is the surety of good things to come. It is the perseverance of all that is integral and impeccable. To behave purely is to be genuine and guileless, a victory for our own virtue. We cannot integrate spirit into our lives without purity. It is a path that cannot be left for an instant. There is a beautiful four step program: Rectify – Don't Deny – Purify – Then Fly!

COWARDLY – heavy emotion
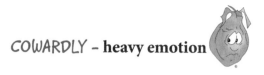

Cowardly: *lack of courage, shamefully fearful, shrinks from trouble.*

Cowardice is the barrier between ourselves and our dreams. It is birthed from low self-esteem and small mindedness. Courage, on the other hand, is the thunder of our beings, arousing and awakening us. The French word "Coeur" means heart. Become a lion heart, a brave heart, being enthralled when encountering the unknown. If at first we don't succeed, we must try and try again. There is no judgment on those who try and fail, only those who fail to try. As long as we keep searching, the answer always comes. Genius does not spring from conformity. It is the product of courageous minds, who dare to act out their most creative dreams, regardless of what others think.

Remember: If one does not feel fear, one cannot feel brave.

⤷ TRANSFORMATION ⤷

COURAGEOUS – light emotion

Courageous: *the quality of mind that enables a person to face difficulties in a brave fashion.*

Dreams cannot be fulfilled without the courage of our convictions. It is a statement of our commitment to ourselves. When we forfeit potential that is waiting to be discovered, we forfeit our predestined future. Courage is the quality of mind which meets challenges with calmness and firmness. It is the ability to be daring, dashing and doubtless.

CRUEL – heavy emotion

Cruel: *disposed to inflict suffering, unreasonable, severe, harsh, hard.*

The word "cruel" has within it the word "rule". Cruelty is birthed by those who want to own the kingdom for themselves. On the other hand, there are those who are cruel to others because they feel owned. Cruelty is the whip that beats the soul. It is time we transformed the sins of the past. If we are ever going to feel any power within ourselves, it is birthed from kindness. Kindness is the antibiotic for the virus of cruelty. Every act of kindness radiates the Divine throughout the entire world. No good deed goes unnoticed. It is said that Heaven is spread beneath the feet of people who are kind. No act of kindness is ever lost; it becomes a part of all the lives it touches.

Remember: Being kind is all the Divine had in mind.

TRANSFORMATION

KIND – light emotion

Kind: *gentle, considerate, benevolent.*

"I shall pass through this world but once
Therefore any good I can do or
Any kindness that I can show
Let me do it now
Let me not defer it nor neglect it
For I shall not pass this way again."
-Mahatma Gandhi

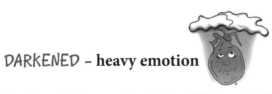

DARKENED - heavy emotion

Darkened: deprived of light, filled with gloom, confusion, blindness.

One of the inroads for the dark is through film and television. We think we get away unscathed, however, our rapid heartbeat and pulse tell us otherwise. The root of darkness is ignorance. It stems from not being able to comprehend the unseen and the unheard. We pay more attention to what we can feel, touch or witness. To understand the contrariness of the dark - live spelled backwards is evil and lived spelled backwards is devil. Darkness is a lack of awareness in our lives; a lack of consciousness from which only error can proceed.

Remember: As Helen Keller said, "The best and most beautiful things in the world cannot be seen or even touched – they must be felt by the heart."

꧁ TRANSFORMATION ꧂

ENLIGHTENED – light emotion

Enlightened: to be free of ignorance, false beliefs or prejudice. To have a spiritual understanding.

Enlightenment comes to those who are willing to be direct, patient, determined and truthful. These attributes are the protection of our innocence and the pathway to our higher intelligence. To be enlightened is to be energetically enrolled in the endless knowledge and possibilities of the Universe. It is an approach that needs no analyzing.

DECEPTIVE – heavy emotion

Deceptive: *the act of fabrication, fraud, lying, trickery, untruth.*

Deceit always involves an injury. It is a pretense of what is not. Where there is a secret, there is no solace. The heart is always impeded by dishonesty. Deceptiveness usually comes from attachment. It comes from a lack of trust that, if we tell the truth, we will not get what we want. If we weren't so attached to it, we would never feel the need to lie about it. Be guided by correct principles, infuse the simple into the complex. Have the faith that whatever is meant to be, will be. The only success that matters is the success that is built on the foundation of us expressing true-ly who we are.

Remember: The most important and pertinent thing in a relationship is the microscopic truth.

➷ TRANSFORMATION ➶

HONEST – light emotion

Honest: *honorable in principles, intentions and actions, sincere, frank.*

Truth is something we must find and honest is something we must be. The saying, "honest to goodness" truth rings true at so many levels. Honesty is the statement of our self respect, which becomes an expression of our Holiness. Words of truth move us into our higher intelligence. They create an aura of trust and honor within ourselves, our family, our community and our world.

DEFEATED – heavy emotion

Defeated: *baffled, beaten, conquered, destroyed, ruined.*

We must never let what we cannot do interfere with what we can do. Statistics show that a great percentage of successful business people have gone through one to three bankruptcies before getting it right. Becoming something new is the success of failure. Defeat may be the truth at the time, however, we had something to learn, to experience, to explore. Never let feeling defeated become a permanent state or become less from it. The difference between defeat and triumph is strictly a point of view. We have the option to see it as a birth of something new that is coming instead of something finished and old. Keep the light switch on, do not turn the electricity off.

Remember: When the going gets tough, the tough get going.

⤳ TRANSFORMATION ⤳

TRIUMPHANT – light emotion

Triumphant: *victory, success.*

Triumph is giving "umph" to trying. It is a victory over the forces of ego. Be an example of perseverance because good examples have twice the value of good advice. Using our creativity to its utmost potential , not being attached to what others think is triumphant. Winning is the ability to feel like a victor no matter what the outcome. It comes with a peace of mind, knowing we did the best we could, we gave it all we had. True triumph is in the trying – not the winning.

DEPRESSED – heavy emotion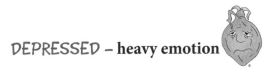

Depressed: *sad, dejected, lowered in position, kept down.*

Depression is usually a reaction to something else, such as, suppressed anger, hurt or defeat. It is our inability to express our hidden feelings. Keeping something to ourselves is a result of needing to be right or heard. Being truthful and not being attached to what others think is an amazing freedom. The road to the best of it, is paved with going through the worst of it. It is so miraculous to feel what the heart desires with no thought of opinion of others. When we stay focused on our own evolvement, we experience an exalted excitement that will not be denied.

Remember: Depression is the suppression of our unique expression.

∾ TRANSFORMATION ∾

EXCITED – light emotion

Excited: *awakened, stimulated, delighted.*

Excitement is an invitation to all that is inspiring. It creates a portal of positivity , power and promise. Excitement comes from doing what we love and loving what we do. It is our birthright to be happy and joyous. When we fully embrace feeling excited, we are refusing to just exist. We act with undue hesitation and exemplify the extraordinary.

DESTRUCTIVE – heavy emotion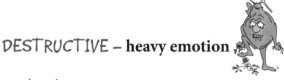

Destructive: *to ruin, to demolish, to annul, to tear down.*

Unfortunately, we live in a world where we witness a tremendous amount of destruction. We are destroying ourselves, each other, the animals and the planet. It is so sad, because we were born to create not destroy. We need to expand our capacity for construction instead of destruction. It is not too late to turn the tides. Let us become endless generators, stimulating and transforming. It is time to be guided by our own creative nature. Deactivate doubt and join with the infinite spiritual current. With each new thing we birth, we become the parent to a better way of life.

Remember: When we create from our soul, no matter how small, we feel a mountain moving through us.

ᑐ TRANSFORMATION ᑐ

CREATIVE – light emotion

Creative: *to cause to come into being, to arrange, to bring about.*

To be creative is to be one with the Creator. We all have the creative genes, we all have creative genius. It is lying dormant, sleeping in a bed of doubt and denial. Creativity is divinity in action, colorfully uniting us with our endless, unlimited potential. Being creative is a powerful force that overturns the tables of despair and depression. It energizes all that is delightful, delicious and deserving….it awakens us to our dreams.

DEVASTATED – heavy emotion

Devastated: *wasted, injured, ravaged.*

Every day of our lives, we hear of something that can devastate us. We are living in a world where the miserable and the miraculous are evolving simultaneously side by side. We must not give in and we must not give up. Masters teach – devastated to activated. "Out of the ashes rises the phoenix". We can be in this world and yet not of it, by educating ourselves to smartly deal with it. Devastation can crush our souls. Therefore, when something devastating happens, we need to quickly, encapsulate, evaluate and elevate.

Remember: One never feels like a captive when one is active.

⤳ TRANSFORMATION ⤳

ECSTATIC – light emotion

Ecstatic: *rapturous delight, poetic inspiration.*

Ecstasy is unclouded joy – it is a bliss that comes from courage and understanding. It is not to be challenged or doubted. When our passion and our purpose meet, we experience an ecstatic feeling that cannot be explained. It is the enrapturing of our existence, where dreams become a reality. When we feel ecstatic, we have gotten rid of the middle man between ourselves and the Universe.

DISAPPOINTED – heavy emotion

Disappointed: *expectations not fulfilled, sense of failure.*

The moment we open ourselves to expectation, we automatically open ourselves to disappointment. Yet, if we do not expect good things for ourselves, we will never have good things for ourselves. Based on the present conditioning of the human race, it is certain that we will experience times of feeling disappointed. Since we cannot eliminate disappointment, we must learn how to deal with it. We need to have a sense of independence, coming from a place of knowing that no matter what, we will manifest what we long for. It is a belief that from every disappointment there is always a new appointment.

Remember: To avoid disappointment use the 4 D's....Detachment, Discernment, Discipline, and Devotion.

⇝ TRANSFORMATION ⇜

DELIGHTED – light emotion

Delighted: *joy, rapture, great pleasure.*

Feeling delighted is the awakening of our divine spark. It is a flaming spiritual force, not to be dampened by anyone or anything. We develop a confidence and conviction. We know, that no matter how dark the situation, the light is not far behind and will always prevail. There is a season, there is a reason, so delight in the journey of the unknown until the time is shown.

DISCOURAGED – heavy emotion

Discouraged: *to feel dispirited and disheartened; prevented by disapproval.*

The word "courage" is within the word "discouraged". In these times, it behooves us to not pay attention to anything that we cannot do anything about. On the other hand, let us pay a great deal of attention to what we can do something about. Let us make a commitment to manifesting our purpose. As long as we keep searching, the answer always comes. There is nothing more important than our ability to consciously question and quest. It will ultimately lead us to the "high" road that we were destined to follow.

Remember: When we realize that nothing has to go right for us to be happy, life becomes so rewarding.

⤳ TRANSFORMATION ⤳

ENCOURAGED – light emotion

Encouraged: *to inspire, to give confidence, to stimulate.*

Encouragement is believing that triumph is indeed the only conclusion to anything we have planned for. We are in the knowing that, no matter what the circumstances, no matter what the outcome, no matter what the timing, all good things will come to us. It comes from our deep belief that for every evil under the sun – thy will be done!

DOUBTING – **heavy emotion**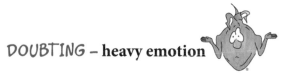

Doubting: *uncertain, undecided, vague, dubious, irresolute.*

When one is doubtful, misfortune is assured. It creates a lack of conviction. It implies a negative evidence. Sometimes, we just have to get out of our own way for a successful path to be cleared. When certainty is bonded to action, we stand in our power. We must be ready at any moment to sacrifice what we are for what we can become. There is no greater achievement than conquering one's doubts. It is living as if we expect our prayers to be answered.

Remember: Doubt diminishes dreams.

∽ TRANSFORMATION ∽

TRUSTING – light emotion

Trusting: *reliance on integrity, confident expectation, hope.*

Whatever the mind can conceive, it can achieve, as long as one believes it so. To think otherwise is false and foolhardy. When we free ourselves from doubt, our lives become divinely quickened because we stop being questioned. Faith comes with trust as trust comes with faith. Trust is a belief without evidence. It comes from an inner knowing that nothing can work with a divided mind.

EGOTISTICAL – heavy emotion

Egotistical: *giving the "I" unique supremacy, self-conceit, self indulgence, disconnected from Source.*

Our ego mind creates illusions, constantly Edging God Out. We become enslaved by our own opinions, losing our connection to our spiritual center. The need to be "right" will always leave us wrong. Ego is never a way back to honor. When we search for something outside ourselves in order to feel whole, it is our ego. When we search for something inside ourselves to feel whole, it is our Holiness. We then lose our minds and find our hearts.

Remember: To be ego-free ….be humble, not arrogant; be embracing, not attacking; be compassionate, not judging; be allowing, not controlling; be flexible, not rigid.

⮜ TRANSFORMATION ⮞

SPIRITUAL – light emotion

Spiritual: *sacred, masterful, soulful.*

The spiritual life is not a theory, it must be lived. A spiritual person often appears as a fool to the eyes of the world, because their ways and rules are very different from the world at large. There is a sense of oneness with the Universal Laws, whereby the journey is about self awareness, self knowledge and self correction. It is an awareness that the destiny of heaven on earth begins and ends with our own personal behavior.

EXHAUSTED – heavy emotion

Exhausted: *tired, worn out, depleted essential ingredients, spent, drained of resources.*

Exhaustion comes from giving too much of our energy away. Unfortunately, in this world, we have an imbalance of takers over givers. Feeling exhausted is the end result of becoming depleted from taking on situations beyond our capacity. Ultimately, this is an oversight of many over-achievers and people-pleasers. Follow the "S" instruction – look for signs, watch for signals, make time for silence and do something sacred.

Remember: The extreme of anything will take the steam out of everything. Equalize to stabilize.

⤸ TRANSFORMATION ⤸

ENERGETIC – light energy

Energetic: *source of usable power, vim, vigor, vitality.*

Everything that happens is based on our energy. It creates our mind's effectiveness, our spirit's electricity and our body's endurance. Our energy is our source, therefore it needs to be guarded, guided and grounded. It is the protection of our soul's happiness and our human giftedness. The power of our light energy field can change the entire world situation, because 1 positive thought transmutes 1,000 negative thoughts.

FEARFUL – **heavy emotion**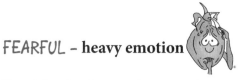

Fearful: *afraid, apprehensive, feeling threatened, uneasy.*

Life is unpredictable and we are all vulnerable to unexpected events. On the one hand, fear can be a lack of faith and on the other hand, it can be a wisdom. Within the word fear is the word ear. We must listen to our inner knowing and intuition. Do not deny feeling afraid but do not dwell on it either. A day of fright can be far more exhausting than a week of work. To every problem there is a solution, just as to every prayer there is an answer. See fear as a challenge rather than an obstacle. Let it motivate us rather than paralyze us. In turn, we become the protector and master of our own domain.

Remember: Very often fear is mind over matter....so if we don't mind....it don't matter.

ꙮ TRANSFORMATION ꙮ

SAFE – light emotion

Safe: *secure, dependable, trustworthy, having faith.*

> When we come to the edge of all the safety we know
> And are about to step into the vast unknown,
> Faith is knowing one of two things will happen;
> There will be something solid to stand on
> Or....we will learn to fly!
> -Author unknown

FRUSTRATED – heavy emotion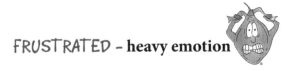

Frustrated: *kept from achieving something, thwarted, blocked.*

Being disconnected from our destiny can leave us feeling extremely frustrated. So often we allow ourselves to be taken off our paths. We relinquish our Divine birthright, our agreement we made with ourselves. If we are not in tune with our own reason for being in this world, it is as if a piece of our life's puzzle is missing. The road to our destiny is always under construction but we must not deviate from our path.

Remember: The 4 P's to our purpose – Plan, Prepare, Proceed and Pursue.

∽ TRANSFORMATION ∽

FULFILLED – light emotion

Fulfilled: *bring to realization, to satisfy, to bring to fruition.*

We all have genius and when it is released, we fulfill our destiny. Destiny is fate foreordained....so let us remember what we are here for. It is not getting what we want that brings fulfillment, it is knowing what we want. Each soul has a job to do, yet each soul must find that job. When our life meets our purpose, it creates an unparalleled feeling, full of enthusiasm and filled with excitement.

GREEDY – heavy emotion

Greedy: *eager to obtain, grasping, insatiable, selfish.*

Today people know the price of everything and more often than not the value of nothing. Greediness is caused by neediness and the neediness of the world is caused by the greediness of the world. We love things and use people, instead of using things and loving people. It is time for us to hold ourselves accountable for the solution. We need to become map makers of a greater awareness, committed to the empowerment and betterment of all. We need to bridge the gap between rich and poor, strong and weak, healthy and sick, educated and non-educated. By doing so, we will coat the Universe with a vibration of miraculous recovery.

Remember: Money will buy a bed but not sleep; a house but not a home; a book but not brains; medicine but not health; amusement but not happiness. It will buy a passport to everywhere but Heaven.

∽ TRANSFORMATION ∽

SHARING – light emotion

Sharing: *to divide, to distribute, to participate jointly.*

Sharing is the solution that can solve all the planet's problems. It creates a karmic ripening, a contribution to the wellness of the world. To share is to make things fair, to make things fair is to care. There is nothing more satisfying than when we are called to the place where our deep gladness and the world's hunger meet. Balancing the scales of injustice bring rewards that are beyond description.

GRIEVING – heavy emotion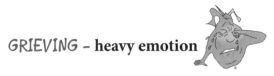

Grieving: *mourning, regretting, sadness, sorrow.*

Grief is the most agonizing emotion of all. Yet, surprisingly, from it stems new beginnings. Most people are afraid to change because they are afraid to grieve. Mourning unrealized becomes the death of happiness. Grief is the ocean that pulls us under, throws us about and spits us out on a new beach....three feet taller. It is the constant reawakening that things are now different. Without grieving, we cannot heal the past, without grieving, we cannot feel the future. It is the representation of our breakdown and our breakthrough. The tears of grief cleanse our soul, making us ready for better ideas to come.

Remember: The relief of grief is turning over a new leaf.

⤳ TRANSFORMATION ⤳

JOYFUL – light emotion

Joyful: *great delight, elation, happiness, pleasure.*

It is our birthright to be joyous and happy. Joy creates a portal of great things happening beyond our wildest imagination. It is the unbridled expression of loving life. To know abundance is to know joy. It is the majestic essence of our beings, a joyous decisiveness of our spirit. To understand the real feeling of joy is to understand the real feeling of freedom.

GUARDED – heavy emotion

Guarded: exhibiting caution, restrained, controlled, defensive.

To be guarded is to be afraid of people, places and things. To guard is to guard against, whereby our hearts and minds become like concrete. Being guarded usually comes from the fear of making mistakes. In truth though, our ability to make mistakes is one of our greatest freedoms. It is the way we learn the lessons of mastery, such as humility, persistence and courage. Mistakes are natural aspects of growth and needed if we are to learn. We must salute them in ourselves and others. Life may be understood backwards, however, it must be lived forwards.

Remember: As Winston Churchill said, "There is no greater fear than fear itself".

∽ TRANSFORMATION ∽

VULNERABLE - light emotion

Vulnerable: capable of receiving attacks, strong enough to receive injuries.

Those who are strong enough to show their vulnerability never grow old. They may die old, but they die young. To allow ourselves to be vulnerable is to allow ourselves to be involved. Without vulnerability, one can neither know their own soul nor touch another's. Vulnerability is knowing we may not always be right, but we are always real. This truly is unquestionable strength of character.

GUILTY – **heavy emotion**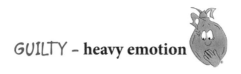

Guilty: *having violated a law; having done wrong.*

Guilt is the annihilator of potential. There is always a "dark" force present, trying to seduce us into doing something that we will feel guilty about. Guilt is the switch that puts out our light. Our creativity gets crushed. However, we are the only ones responsible for this atrocity. No one can make us feel guilty if we have nothing to feel guilty about. If our intentions are coming from a place of purity, our life is protected, no matter what the outcome.

Remember: Mahatma Gandhi's Seven Sins that create a guilt-filled life:

Wealth without work
Knowledge without character
Commerce without morality
Science without humanity
Worship without sacrifice
Politics without principles

↪ TRANSFORMATION ↩

GUILTLESS – light emotion

Guiltless: *innocent, pure, devoid of guilt.*

Onionhead®'s Seven attributes that create a guilt-free life:

Heart
Honesty
Humility
Honor
High-mindedness
Hard working
and of course....Humor!

HARSH – heavy emotion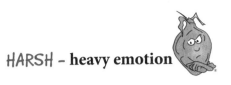

Harsh: *rough to the senses, disagreeable, irritating, hard.*

Harshness is sandpaper to the soul. Feeling whole is when our personality and our soul walk hand in hand. The soul knows nothing of being hard and cruel. It stems from an entity outside of ourselves. This usually is triggered from the feeling of "being taken advantaged of". However, when we realize nothing has to go right for us to be okay, then no one can steal our harmony. We develop a power that knows no barriers and has no intimidating beliefs. We awaken the gentle giant that lives within us.

Remember: Better to leave harsh words unspoken than to have to mend the hearts they have broken.

TRANSFORMATION

GENTLE – light emotion

Gentle: *noble, considerate, generously inclined.*

Being a steward of life is living gently. It is the one attribute that can diffuse any harsh situation. When in doubt or confusion, think gently, speak gently and behave gently. The gentle word, more often than not, turneth away anger. It is like water to a fire. In olden times a gentle knight was known as a chivalrous knight because his kindness was considered extremely noble. There is no accident that we are called....gentle-men and gentle-women.

HATEFUL – heavy emotion

Hateful: *intense aversion, animosity, malignity, detesting.*

Whatever we put out, we will get back. So we must be careful about the feeling of hate because it surely will be returned to us. Don't denounce it, but don't announce it. This negative passion can certainly spur us on to making a difference. After all, there are many detestable things happening in this world, such as child abuse, animal abuse, planet abuse and government abuse. The Holiest place is where a hatred becomes a love. Our hatred of something can become the catalyst for us creating something wonderfully loving.

Remember: Let's have our hate become the bait to change someone else's or our own horrible fate.

∽ TRANSFORMATION ∽

LOVING – light emotion

Loving: *fondness, heartfelt regard, to delight in, to take pleasure in.*

Love is the yearning or outgoing of the soul towards something that is regarded as wonderful and wondrous. In its full sense, it denotes something deeply spiritual. Love is everything and without it we are nothing. One single act of love bears the imprint of heaven on earth. Stay loyal to love, it leaves an indelible mark of mastery on our life's record. Quite simply.... be loving – beloved.

HEARTLESS – heavy emotion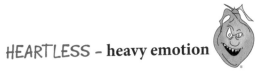

Heartless: *without sympathy, without affection, lacking kindness.*

When we shut down our heart, we shut down our soul. We were never meant to be mean. The heart of the problem is always a problem of the heart. We deny our own divinity. Something does not hurt any less just because we pretend it doesn't. To know our own heart is to know many things. It is our love intelligence which leads to the birthing of our compassion. There is only ONE pathway to peace and it is through the heart. When we follow our heart, our happiness follows.

Remember: To be heartless is to be soul homeless...crying out loud atrocity.

∽ TRANSFORMATION ∽

COMPASSIONATE – light emotion

Compassionate: *charitable, sympathetic, humane, caring, heartfelt.*

There is nothing higher than compassion. It is the chariot for our souls. We become understanding, undivided and universally united. Being compassionate is a devotion to the undefended. It comes from a deep yearning to help our fellow man. Mother Teresa once said, "If people of the world would source their compassion, we would have no suffering of poverty". Com-passion is our commitment to our passion.

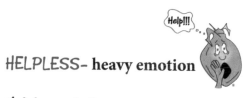

HELPLESS- **heavy emotion**

Helpless: *feeling incompetent, incapable, feeble, ineffective, powerless.*

Helplessness many times is at the root of anger, frustration and grief. It is our inability to connect with our power. It is as if there is a room divider between ourselves and our potential. As children, the feeling of helplessness is painful and frustrating. Unfortunately, we take these emotions into our adulthood. Our soul needs to be re-aligned and our power needs to be ignited. It is a potent journey, based on intelligence, intuition and integrity. People who gain victory over external difficulties are strong; but people who gain victory over their own internal difficulties are all powerful.

Remember: The less we help – the more help-less we feel.

⌇ TRANSFORMATION ⌇

POWERFUL - light emotion

Powerful: *possessing great force, strong, efficient, having great energy.*

The power of love is the power of life. Most people judge power in relationship to something outside themselves, but truly, it is a force that is within themselves. It is a passion that comes from the yearning of the soul. It is detached, defined, definite and Divine.

> "DID is a word of achievement
> WON'T is a word of retreat
> MIGHT is a word of bereavement
> OUGHT is a word of duty
> TRY is a word of each hour
> WILL is a word of beauty
> CAN is a word of power"
> -Author unknown

HOPELESS – heavy emotion

Hopeless: *despairing, despondent, desperate, sense of futility.*

Hopelessness is the "what's the use….nothing will work anyway and no one really loves me" syndrome. All of us have felt this at one time or another. It is a feeling that causes agony to the heart and trauma to the soul. More often than not, this is the root feeling that causes feelings of suicide. A person who is not capable of loving us, or a business whose time has not come, or even a government that overlooks its people can cause a sense of hopelessness. We must not allow others to invade our sense of wellness. The key is to not give up, instead....look up!

Remember: As Oliver Holmes said, "What lies behind us and what lies before us are tiny matters compared to what lies within us."

⤳ TRANSFORMATION ⤳

HOPEFUL – light emotion

Hopeful: *to trust, to feel excited, to anticipate, to be filled with promise.*

Hope is the source of real innocence. It is a statement of childlike excitement, not letting any doubt of this world interfere. Life is just a journey and traveling hopefully is even better than arriving. The ability of the mind to make substance out of ideas is called hope. Thomas Edison made over 5,000 attempts before he discovered the right filament for the light bulb. Being ready to do everything we were told could not be done is birthed from our heartfelt hope.

HORRIBLE – **heavy emotion**

Horrible: *causing a feeling of horror, terrible, dreadful, shocking, ugly.*

No one deserves the ache of feeling horrified. It leaves an indelible mark upon our soul. Therefore, it is extremely important to relieve our systems and release these feelings. Not released, the heart can become hardened and the soul is left feeling harnessed. No one can feel horrible without cause. Our cries must not be silenced, they are the first step to change and transformation. We all have the strength to overcome any obstacles that stand in our way. It may be long ride but it is a trip worth taking.

Remember: Do not repress....do not suppress....express....it releases stress....changes the mess....then we feel blessed!

↪ TRANSFORMATION ↩

WONDERFUL – light emotion

Wonderful: *of an exciting nature, marvelous, wondrous, miraculous.*

Provoking awe and wonder in our lives transforms us utterly. It is the rapture of life. To live in wonder is to live in enlightenment. It is an avenue which takes us to the path of pleasure and promise. When our soul and our personality walk hand in hand, our life is full of wonder. When feeling horrible, something has happened and yet nothing has to happen for us to feel wonderful.

HUMILIATED – heavy emotion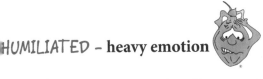

Humiliated: *pride offended, self-respect lowered, dignity degraded, integrity challenged.*

Nothing is worse than feeling humiliated. It steamrolls the heart and crushes the soul. It is sad indeed that many people empower themselves by humiliating others. It is doubtful if there is one person who has escaped this horror. However, we are called upon to examine how we humiliate ourselves. We cannot control the events in our lives, but we can control how we react to them. We must temper our tempers. Let us be careful in our words for they can be the determinant of our lives.

Remember: As Eleanor Roosevelt said, "no one can make you feel inferior without your consent".

⤳ TRANSFORMATION ⤳

HONORED – light emotion

Honored: *respectability, credibility, good, honest, moral.*

Believe in honor and life will be honorable. Believe in respect and life will be respectable. To be respected and honored is more important to our soul than being loved. It is the stepping stone to all that is worthwhile. Let us reach above to help ourselves and reach below to help another. There will be some ahead of us and some behind us, however all that really matters is what lies within us. To be honorable is to follow the 4 T's – truthful, trust worthy, timely and tender.

IGNORANT - **heavy emotion**

Ignorant: *lack of knowledge, lack of awareness, lack of experience.*

Ignorance is our planet's most formidable enemy. Evil is birthed from ignorance. People do not realize how their bad behavior affects the whole world. All life is connected; when one part is damaged, everything else is affected. Ignorance is to ignore, to ignore is not to see. When we are blinded to what ills are happening around us, we do not participate in its healing. If we are not part of the solution, we are part of the problem. It is time for us to hold ourselves accountable for the wellness, not only of ourselves, but for the whole world around us. Ignorance can only be overcome by putting our wisdom to practical use.

Remember: Wisdom is evaluating experiences of the past which ensures a better future.

⤳ TRANSFORMATION ⤳

WISE - light emotion

Wise: *to know the true facts, prudent, sensible.*

We can buy an education but wisdom is the ability to go deep within and find the source that comes from an ancient knowing. It is not learned – it is a birthright. To be wise is a discipline to not give in to mediocre behavior. It is accountability – the ability to account for the truth of something. There is a difference between knowledge and wisdom – knowledge is something we acquire – wisdom is a gift that comes from something higher.

IMPATIENT – heavy emotion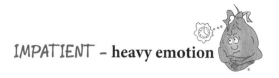

Impatient: *annoyance because of delay, restless eagerness, opposition, intolerance, pettiness.*

Only when we move at the pace of the Universe, will life flow effortlessly. There are three keys to the door of Heaven – practice, perseverance and patience. Practice is the easiest, perseverance the most demanding and patience the most difficult. Impatience is the hunger for the end result. This attitude yields inaccurate information and therefore leads to misfortune. When we come to understand that we are but one small piece of a very large puzzle, we then realize that everything has its own timing.

Remember: Patience is a willingness to accept whatever the future holds, without trying to change Great Spirit's plan.

⤳ TRANSFORMATION ⤳

PATIENT – light emotion

Patient: *tolerant, tender, tranquil, ability to await events without agitation.*

Patience is the soul's quietude. It is a virtue that expresses flexibility and sustainability. Being unaffected by delays gives way to the summoning of miracles. It allows the Universal Plan to unfold as intended, without needing proof of such. Patience is an ACTIVE force denoting uncomplaining steadiness. This, in itself, facilitates an awareness of the unannounced. Being patient is the proclamation of our professionalism.

IMPRISONED - heavy emotion

Imprisoned: *restricted, limited, confined.*

The left brain is the logical, practical side of the brain. It, more often than not, chains the right brain, which is the creative, spiritual side of the brain. One does not have to be in jail to feel imprisoned. Most of the time, in fact, we imprison ourselves. Imprisonment is a potpourri of poisonous thoughts of scarcity and low self esteem. This, in turn, prevents us from seeing the truth of our magnificence. Freedom comes from knowing that life provides the canvas and we do the painting. We are the artists who can create whatever we want.

Remember: Take the risk, it is better than forfeiting our freedom.

↜ TRANSFORMATION ↜

FREE - light emotion

Free: *independent, unconfined, unimpeded, unrestrained.*

To feel free is to be free. It is a state of mind. Nelson Mandela felt free when he was imprisoned because he treasured what he believed in. Yet others are free to do whatever they want and yet they feel chained to the disappointments of life. Freedom is written on our hearts. It is our heartfelt connection to our relationships, work or causes. We become free agents for ourselves, unimpeded, unobstructed and therefore unhindered. We do not let what we cannot do stand in the way of what we can do. Choice, not chance, determines our destiny.

INSENSITIVE – heavy emotion

Insensitive: *deprived of sensitivity, devoid of compassion, irritating to the senses of others.*

In our harsh reality, we become desensitized in order to survive. However, this is the root of all violence. It is only when we realize how much something hurts us that we are unwilling to hurt another. If we cannot learn from the problem, we become the problem. We need to wake up our senses to come to our senses. Without sensitivity, we are condemned to the unconsciousness that wounds. In hurting another, we inevitably harm ourselves.

Remember: Always be kinder than necessary....it is the pathway to our peace.

⤷ TRANSFORMATION ⤶

SENSITIVE – light emotion

Sensitive: *wise, sensible, caring, empathetic.*

Being sensitive is an openness to clear communication. To hear the whispered voice of another's heart and understand their unspoken words are the talents of very few. Love blossoms when we are sensitive to another person's need. It seals the relationship in honesty and humility. Through our sensitivity we become more perceptive, more aware and undeniably more sensible.

IRRESPONSIBLE – heavy emotion

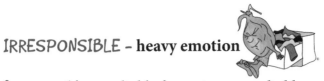

Irresponsible: *not liable for actions, unreliable, careless of responsibilities.*

We live in a world that leans towards the "I" program. Where there is no admittance of responsibility, there is a trail left behind of wounded souls. Many things may not be comfortable but they are necessary. As individuals or as a collective team, we must learn to carry things out to the very end. We are responsible for what happens in the future, no matter what has happened in our past. We need to take it back to make it right. In truth, it is the biggest gift we can give to ourselves.

Remember: Nothing keeps a person's feet on the ground like having a responsibility placed on their shoulders.

⤳ TRANSFORMATION ⤳

RESPONSIBLE – light emotion

Responsible: *answerable, ethical, dutiful, accountable.*

When a problem arises, we must look at our own responsibility in it. When we blame someone else, we give them our power. Sometimes we are responsible for others and sometimes, we are responsible to others. We all enrolled in this full-time job called life, where there are rules and there are consequences. If we would all take responsibility for the planet's pain, we would eliminate war and poverty. The noblest inspirations are worthless without taking the responsibility for them.

ISOLATED- heavy emotion

Isolated: *detached, separated, set apart from, alone.*

It seems as if we are all in this together....separated. Each one of us has our own mission, purpose and destiny and yet if we do not join and intermingle, we will never find it. We must constantly search for ways to unite with our fellow man. One can go alone, but one cannot grow alone. Relationships are our greatest teachers. People are brought to us not to change us but to give us an opportunity to change. They are our education that takes us to a better understanding of who we are and why we are here.

Remember: Snowflakes are the most fragile things of all but look what they can do when they stick together.

∽ TRANSFORMATION ∽

CONNECTED – light emotion

Connected: *to join together, to associate, to unite.*

To feel a connectedness is to feel a consciousness. It facilitates the awakening of our heart and the arousing of our intellect. Connecting is contributing to the sanctity of our species. It is a statement of aliveness not aloneness, cooperation not competition and divinity not division. It expands our capacity to be enlightened and enlivened. Achievement without connection is meaningless.

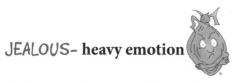

JEALOUS- **heavy emotion**

Jealous: *envious, resentful, suspicious, apprehensive of being replaced, gee lousy.*

It is a common scarcity belief that there is not enough for everyone. Therefore, it leaves us with a sense of guardianship over what we want to be ours. It leaves us watchful, maybe even a little paranoid. Before we know it, we are no longer happy for others. Even worse, before we know it, we are no longer happy for ourselves. In truth, there is enough of everything....for everybody. The most rewarding aspects of life can be seen and felt when we loyally support the goals of others. By fostering altruistic motives, we bring honor and respect to our own life. Faith is a fabulous remedy to jealousy.

Remember: There are as many paths to enrichment as there are beings in the Universe.

⌒ TRANSFORMATION ⌒

EMBRACING - light emotion

Embracing: *to include, to avail oneself, to encompass, to hold.*

"One who saves a single life saves the entire world".
-The Talmud

"God loves us all equally and has no favorite children".
-The Bible

"Enlightenment comes from being detached and embracing all outcome outside of ourselves."
-Buddhist Teaching

JUDGING – heavy emotion

Judging: *to form an opinion, to be critical of, to cheapen.*

It is wise to judge situations but it is wicked to judge people. When we judge others we do not love others. Likewise, when we judge ourselves, we do not love ourselves. The truth is we all came here just to have a better understanding of ourselves and others. Judging critically comes from assuming something and is funded through ignorance. Understanding comes from studying something and is founded through intelligence. Beliefs without knowledge must be revised.

Remember: Use better judgment – don't judge!

⤳ TRANSFORMATION ⤳

UNDERSTANDING – light emotion

Understanding: *to know the meaning of, to comprehend, to perceive, to solve.*

Understanding comes from an enlightened understanding of differences. Without it, we cannot heal the past for ourselves or others. Understanding is developed from our ability to talk in a way so others can listen and listen in a way so others can talk. It is the knowledge that listening requires more than just being quiet. It is an intention to learn more in order to love better.

LETHARGIC – **heavy emotion**

Lethargic: *apathetic, dull, drowsy, no energy.*

Lethargy is a lethal weapon against our divinity. There are usually one thousand reasons why we should not do something and ten reasons why we should. It is the way darkness reigns over our light. The blossoming mind will wither if it does not keep being inspired. He who has no fire will always be tired. We need to keep our ideals alive, knowing that as long as we keep searching, our destiny will be found. This, in itself will energize and crystallize our creative forces.

Remember: Believe in nothing and life will be empty.

∽ TRANSFORMATION ∽

DETERMINED – light emotion

Determined: *to be committed, to be strong, to be willed.*

Determination is what differentiates leaders from dreamers. It is a will that will not wither. Life is full of challenges and obstacles. Therefore, we need a force within ourselves and a belief greater than ourselves. Our determination is what keeps us in alignment with our predestined fate. It carries us through all doubt and despair. We then live by acting, not by thinking about acting. Our internal dialogue is disciplined and decisive. This one attribute will lead us to self knowledge , self confidence and self realization.

LIMITED - heavy emotion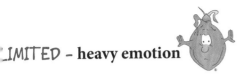

Limited: confined, restricted, narrow, narrow minded.

As a race, we seem more comfortable limiting ourselves. We are hesitant to think outside the box. This keeps us from all the wonder and marvel that is just waiting to be discovered. Miracles do in fact happen, we just have to believe in them. Every important discovery happened because someone had the courage to think limitlessly, with no constraints, just convictions. For a true believer, there is nothing that cannot be done.

Remember: The destiny of heaven on earth begins and ends with our own personal belief system.

ꙶ TRANSFORMATION ꙶ

UNLIMITED - light emotion

Unlimited: unbounded, endless, exceptional, undefined.

When we are one with our Divine spark, we have unlimited potential. Life becomes exquisite, whereby miracles become an every day occurrence. Our creativity uses the insignificant to accomplish the impossible. We become what we wished for and we manifest what we hoped for. The Universe is our playground and we become one with our majestic magnificence.

LONELY – **heavy emotion**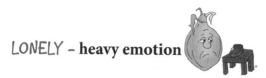

Lonely: *deserted, secluded, friendless.*

There is a difference between alone and lonely. On the one hand, we should always be striving for our uniqueness and our ability to stand alone. On the other hand, we cannot find our uniqueness and independence without the teachings from another. Through relationship, we learn about interdependence. It is not a co-dependence whereby, we feel we need the other person in order to survive. A healthy relationship is one, whereby we know we can achieve more together than we can alone. It is built on the mutual recognition of virtue and a mutual acceptance of differences.

Remember: Succeeding alone means we have survived; succeeding with other means we have truly lived.

∽ TRANSFORMATION ∽

LOVED – light emotion

Loved: *deep tenderness, devotion, delight in.*

Feeling loved can override all heavy feelings. The smallest act of love is more than every other work put together. Without love there is an emptiness that knows no solace. With love there is a fulfillment that knows no sorrow. To love for the sake of being loved is human – to love for the sake of loving is enlightenment.

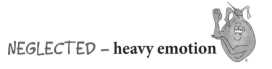

NEGLECTED – heavy emotion

Neglected: *disregarded, ignored, slighted, lack of proper care.*

Our world's children, our world's animals and our world herself are all dying from neglect. It is an atrocity that needs to be reckoned with. It is time to defend all that is beautiful. We must make a commitment to protect what we can, wherever we can, whenever we can. If we are not protected as individuals, we are not protected as a race. When one of us suffers, we all suffer. If we do not use our power, we will lose our power. It is time for Heaven and Earth to stop being separate countries.

Remember: Prepare a better world for a future to come.

∽ TRANSFORMATION ∽

PROTECTED – light emotion

Protected: *to shield, to defend, to guard.*

While looking to protect another, we must make certain we are protected ourselves. To protect does not mean to sacrifice, it means to justify. It comes from an consciousness of concern. To be protected is to be safe, to be safe is to be proactive. Asking for protection is the beginning of receiving and giving protection is the beginning of rewards.

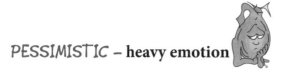

PESSIMISTIC – **heavy emotion**

Pessimistic: *expecting the worst, a belief that evil outweighs good, to expect misfortune.*

Life is what we expect it to be. Our thoughts are our best friends or our worst enemies. It is the darkness verses the light. Working with a pessimistic mind always gives results that are less than hoped for. However, we can be benefitted by using external difficulties as tools for our own advancement. Problems and difficulties are just eye openers. They teach us to break the illusions that we created to appease our own attachments.

Remember: When we free ourselves from pessimism, we free ourselves from darkness.

↬ TRANSFORMATION ↫

OPTIMISTIC – light emotion

Optimistic: *looking on the bright side, belief in the positive, the doctrine that everything is for the best.*

Optimism leads to our power that is funded from the Universal Realm. It creates an opening that transforms the abused into the beautiful and a difficulty into a divinity. When we feel optimistic, our hearts flutter, our souls sing and our life takes flight. We grab a greater vision, manifest a larger mission and find a peace within ourselves that cannot be explained…. because it is too extraordinary.

REJECTED – heavy emotion

Rejected: *not believed, cast off, passed over, discarded.*

Rejection feels like a knife wound to the heart. It leaves us feeling unwanted, disrespected, dishonored and unloved. However, we do have the choice to change our views. When we are not at the whim of what others think, we develop within ourselves a knowingness of our own self respect and self worth. There is so much competition on this earth plane. Competing is extremely challenging because there always has to be a loser, someone is always rejected. Cooperation, on the other hand, creates a winning space for all, because the many work for the one idea, cause or goal.

Remember: Rejection can sometimes be an intervention from the Divine because unbeknownst to us, we were on the wrong path.

⇜ TRANSFORMATION ⇝

ACCEPTED – light emotion

Accepted: *agreed upon, acknowledged, endorsed, recognized, believed.*

All of us want to feel accepted. It is the acknowledgement of our being, a validity of our value. However, needing this from others can also leave us vulnerable to heartache. Though it is true that being accepted is better than being rejected, when inspected....it can be detected that it merely reflected, we were gloriously protected!

RESENTFUL – heavy emotion

Resentful: *showing displeasure, showing indignation, feeling offended or abused.*

Resentment hardens the heart. It births a selfishness and self-indulgence, which becomes the death of our happiness and joy. Resenting something or someone is a poison that must be cleaned out. We have a responsibility to ourselves not to be a carrier of this disease. To clean is to clear, therefore, the only way to heal resentment is through forgiveness. We then create an energy of "rising above" and "going beyond". We come to believe that problems arise in our lives because we need their lessons.

Remember: As resentment is an earlier hell, forgiveness is an earlier heaven.

↭ TRANSFORMATION ↭

FORGIVING – light emotion

Forgiving: *merciful, charitable, compassionate, pardoning.*

Forgiveness is the manna of life. It unlocks all doors to the subconscious and awakens us to our limitless potential. The most generous gift we can give to ourselves is our ability to forgive. It softens all hardness, whether that be in ourselves or another. The more we forgive, the safer we are. The happiest relationships are the union of two forgivers. When we forgive, we fore go all heaviness so we are totally free to fly.

RIGID – heavy emotion

Rigid: *resisting change, inflexible, hard.*

To be rigid is to be like ice – cold and immovable. Rigidity comes from fear of something. It could be fear of change, fear of loss, or fear of something new. Whatever the case, it calls for transformation. Let us be subtle, not stubborn; observing, not obstinate; receptive, not aggressive; open, not closed. When our nature reflects these attributes, it affects everyone and everything around us. The bamboo shoot is a perfect example. It has a longer life span than most plants because it does not stand hard against the elements. It bends with the wind, making it invulnerable to break.

Remember: When rigid, we feel a death of sorts – when flexible, we affirm greater life.

∽ TRANSFORMATION ∽

FLEXIBLE – light emotion

Flexible: *pliable, yielding, compliant, capable of bending without breaking.*

Flexibility is our ability to be flexible. We are able to comfortably arrange whatever pieces come our way. This is because flexibility comes with trust, as trust comes with flexibility. It awakens our curiosity and curiosity is the path to eternal youth. It is a fabulous formula for expansion, expression, excitement and external forces that want to play a role in our life.

SAD – heavy emotion

Sad: *sorrowful, depressed in spirit, gloomy, unhappy, mournful.*

Sadness not recognized is a doorway to depression. Anger, more times than not, is a reaction to unresolved sadness. However, sadness is an emotion that must not be repressed. We all have good reasons to feel sad. We are constantly being bombarded with stories that are completely heartbreaking and heart wrenching. Our sadness is our statement of things we want to be different and of things that are not acceptable. Actually, feeling sad is a sign of wholeness and strength. It is what instigates change. Sadness unleashed is the opening for compassion, consciousness and charity.

Remember: A smile gladdens the heart – a frown saddens the heart.

ᔌ TRANSFORMATION ᔌ

HAPPY – light emotion

Happy: *contented, delighted, blessed, filled with bliss, comforted, joyful.*

Most smiles start with another smile. To feel happy is to feel heaven. The highest form of mastery is sense of humor. It is the oil that lubricates all friction. Our souls love laughter and it serves as the jumper cable for our hearts. Contentment is not the absence of problems but the ability to deal with them. True happiness is founded in right action and right action is founded in holiness.

SCATTERED – **heavy emotion**

Scattered: *without concentration, dispersed, squandered, flighty, frivolous.*

We live in a world where we are inundated with too many options and too much information. It is no wonder we get scattered and lose our way. We become distanced from our destiny. The answer is in staying centered, simple and grounded. We need to take ourselves seriously and choose carefully. Our choices today are what create our future tomorrow. We need to be discerning and disciplined. This facilitates an undivided mind.

Remember: Always begin by having the end in mind.

↬ TRANSFORMATION ↫

FOCUSED – light emotion

Focused: *concentrated, meet with intention.*

Focus is what creates success. By focusing on something, we energize it. We are clear, precise and unconfused. We have within us the power to do whatever we want, even if it has not been done before. When we have a certainty, it means something certain is about to happen. All men and women of greatness had one thing in common. They were focused, firm and futuristic. If we want to become first rate, we must first become focused. We then make our life an example for all to follow.

SELFISH – **heavy emotion**

Selfish: *caring for one's own interest only, self-indulgent, self-involved, narcissistic.*

To be selfish is to be sinful. It is what has created our world of "haves" and "have nots". With the incredible amount of abundance on this earth plane, there is no reasonable excuse for hunger of any sort. Blessings must be shared, not owned. To give unselfishly is to coat the world with a vibration of victory. The truly generous realize that we ensure our divine destiny by what we give, not by what we get.

Remember: Being selfish creates a sea of sorrow, where there is no solace.

⟿ TRANSFORMATION ⟿

GENEROUS – light emotion

Generous: *bountiful, chivalrous, free, magnanimous, noble.*

Giving is its own reward. It is the acknowledgement of our enlightenment. It is love put into action. In the life of the generous, funding is always available. Childlike behavior is put away and chivalry is awakened. Every time we care, we extinguish indifference. Generosity produces a wave of wellness, whereby our goodness is focused on the good for all.

STRESSED – heavy emotion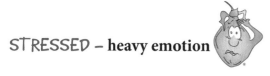

Stressed: *pressured, stretched to the limit, tense, strained.*

No matter what the object, when stretched too far - it breaks. As humans, we are no different. The way we manifest and express our energy determines the quality of our life. We are all unique, so we need to create the pace for ourselves that is in alignment with our own rhythm. We need to set our own timing. Life is filled with difficulty and disappointment. We cannot avoid this disturbance but we do not have to avail it either. Cultivating our own correctness is a crucial step to our own contentment.

Remember: When we stress, we second guess, we make a mess and then we end up with less.

⤷ TRANSFORMATION ⤶

CALM - light emotion

Calm: *free from disturbance, serene, at peace, stillness.*

We must stay calm to reach our center, where our mindfulness lies. In this world we live in, trouble is bound to come, so cultivating our calmness is extremely important. By staying calm, we avoid calamity. Calmness comes from a sense of knowing that all will work out; it is just a matter of time. It stems from an awareness that there is, indeed, a Universal Plan and we are but one small part of it. Calmness creates a sense of simplicity to all complexities.

STUBBORN – **heavy emotion**

Stubborn: *inflexible, unreasonable, obstinate, not easily handled.*

We cannot learn anything when we are stubborn. It is cement for our creativity and nothing can grow from concrete. We are here in this world for self-development and self-cultivation. Stubbornness retards that process. Do not confuse stubbornness, which is a self-righteous, from firmness, which is self-respect. When we are stubborn, we have the need to be right; when we are firm, we affirm a greater knowledge or higher wisdom.

Remember: Stubbornness is a sign of weakness imitating strength.

∽ TRANSFORMATION ∽

WILLING – light emotion

Willing: *strong determination, practical enthusiasm, direct effort.*

To be willing is an openness that embraces the experiences of life's journey. It is an intelligence that comes from intuition and inspiration. Willingness is an invitation to our unlimited potential, leaving the controls to the unfolding of things to come. Wishes become realities through willpower not wish power. Willing to become something new is the path of the spiritual warrior.

UNCONSCIOUS – heavy emotion

UnConscious: to be unaware, to not be mindful, not cognizant.

To be unconscious is to be half alive. We dull our senses. We lose our sensitivity and our common sense. We "zone out" and do not even notice what is happening around us. It is imperative that we awaken ourselves to our consciousness. It is connected to our master within. There is an urgency for us to wake up and become part of a higher intelligence. Corruption, abuse, cheating, starvation, dishonesty and, even death come from unconsciousness. As Einstein said, "No problem can be solved from the same level of consciousness that created it".

Remember: to be unconscious is similar to lack of conscience.

∽ TRANSFORMATION ∽

CONSCIOUS – light emotion

Conscious: to be aware, to be knowledgeable, to be intellectually involved.

Consciousness is an energy that is connected to our internal wisdom and our external awareness. It is a statement of our enlightenment. To be conscious is to be in touch with our circumstances and their origin. It is a forceful energy that can remedy any situation. Through being conscious, we bring clarity to confusion and peace to problems. We bring order to chaos and wrongs become righted. We manifest the answer we were seeking because we awaken our senses and sensibility.

UNDISCIPLINED – heavy emotion

Undisciplined: *to be untrained, disobedient, unruly.*

Being undisciplined creates an atmosphere of chaos that prevents positive results from manifesting. It is a fast track to nowhere. Do not underestimate the power of discipline. Lack of it is the number one reason why we fail at things. We did not have the wherewithal to stay the course, ride the wave or keep the belief. Discipline is the vital force that activates transformation. Through it, we take the risk, we do what is right and we reap the rewards.

Remember: To be undisciplined is to be undeserving.

TRANSFORMATION

DISCIPLINED – light emotion

Disciplined: *trained, educated, obedient, honoring.*

The most worthwhile intentions are worthless without discipline. Discipline is the commitment to all that is worthy. It paves the way for us to reach our predestined goals and dreams. It is a course of evaluation, education and elevation. It is a willingness to take rebuke, self-correct and become enthralled with what we have become.

UNGRATEFUL – **heavy emotion** 

Ungrateful: *not showing thanks, not showing gratitude, denying blessings.*

Feeling ungrateful leaves us feeling empty and sorrow filled. It is the denial of what is good in our lives. It is a betrayal to our happiness. All sadness and regret are washed whiter then snow when we are in a grateful frame of mind. When we focus on what we do not have instead of what we do have, we leave out all that Heaven was trying to gift us with. Worse yet, when we feel ungrateful, we forget to honor another and even more disturbing....we forget to honor ourselves.

Remember: Let us forget what we have given and remember what we have received.

TRANSFORMATION

GRATEFUL – light emotion 

Grateful: *thankful, delightful, agreeable, pleased.*

When we feel grateful, we feel great! It is the unveiling of self-centered ego and simultaneously helps us make the most of ourselves. It is the emotion that sheds all that is impure. We begin to see obstacles as opportunities, grateful for the lessons. Gratitude is the victory of defeat. This, in itself, becomes a sealing of our good fortune, securing a grand future.

UNLUCKY – **heavy emotion**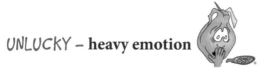

Unlucky: *unfortunate, ill-omened, not favored.*

We do not have luck, we make luck. It is all in our attitude. However, in our world today, it is true that bad things can happen to good people. This is unfortunate but not unlucky. Masters say that the harder we work, the luckier we get. When we serve with the higher elements, we start to reign over the lower elements. Then our energetic field shifts and we become more in alignment with the Universal Realm.

Remember: Luck is the result of:

Love – Understanding – Consciousness – Kindness

≈ TRANSFORMATION ≈

LUCKY – light emotion

Lucky: *good fortune, blessed, favorable, delightful.*

Luck comes from knowing that our good choices today determine our better tomorrow. Our hearts always have the first answer. If we do what we love, blessings will follow. Our luck comes from daring to be the difference that makes the difference. We then become the luck we were looking for. It is well known that the Universe always gives to the giver an unbounded reservoir of riches.

VIOLENT – heavy emotion

Violent: *raging, furious, rough, vehemently forceful.*

The act of violence never has an excuse. The only way to stop the violence in the world is to stop the violence in ourselves. We must become conscious of our words. For example, "oh I could kill you" or "I could murder you" or "kill two birds with one stone" are all said innocently, yet they create a wave of very dark energy. We have the power to transmute all this darkness into the light...it is just a matter of becoming more conscious. We can be the difference between what was and what is to come.

Remember: Violence tears up Heaven's rewards by its roots.

≈ TRANSFORMATION ≈

PEACEFUL - light emotion

Peaceful: *free from disturbance, tranquil, serene, calm, spiritually content.*

Those who love peace must learn to work as effectively as those who love war. We can give somebody a "peace" of our mind, without ever losing our mind. Fight rage with righteousness, meanness with meaning and anger with awareness. Then life becomes a "peace" of cake, deliciously stimulating and ever so rewarding. Always believe that world peace is indeed the only conclusion.

WORRIED – **heavy emotion**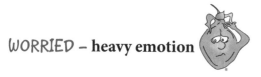

Worried: *uneasy, troubled, anxious.*

Worry costs a lot and accomplishes nothing. Worrying takes a toll on our spirit. It disconnects us from what is well and wonderful. There is an answer to every problem. If we center ourselves and call upon our higher wisdom, the solution will inevitably reveal itself. The only time we need be worried is if we created something in our lives that was not prudent, honest, or safe. Our impeccability and integrity are our best protection against worry because they guide us to our wellness.

Remember: Worry is the weapon between ourselves and our wonder.

TRANSFORMATION

ENTHUSIASTIC – light emotion

Enthusiastic: *exalted, eager, excited, divine will.*

Enthusiasm is the fire that gives power to any endeavor. Enthusiastic is derived from the Greek word "enthu", which means "in God". When we are enthusiastic, we are in a state of oneness with the Universe and its limitless potential. We are released from all entrapments. We have activated our divine spark, our uniqueness, our individuality, our purpose, our reason for being. We are IN LOVE!

WOUNDED - heavy emotion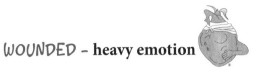

Wounded: *hurt, injured, bruised, pained, traumatized.*

There is not a soul in this world who has not been wounded at one time or another. As a society, we want to numb ourselves and put ourselves to sleep. We cannot see a way out. However, the good news is, when we lose our minds, we come to our senses. When we finally name our wounds, we finally let them go. Healing is available to all who avail themselves to it. Healing is also available to all who help others heal. It is the law of the Universe.

Remember: Feel the feeling - peel the feeling - heal the feeling - seal the healing.

∽ TRANSFORMATION ∽

HEALED – light emotion

Healed: *to be well, to be cured, to remedy, to make healthy again.*

Healing comes as a result of love. Loving others heals two wounds, theirs and ours. Love conquers all that stands in its way, it is a divine force that is unstoppable and unbeatable. Love is a potion, a patent, a promise, a peace. With love, we are everything and without it, we are nothing. The soul knows no other reason for being....than to love....and love....and love....and love.

The end is only the beginning. The healing of ourselves is the birthing of a new world, where love and light reign. If every one of us makes a committed effort to our own healing and then commits to helping others heal, we will know a paradise, that we thought only possible in our dreams. We will remember that as human souls, though we are so different, we are all the same.

The ambassadors to world peace,

The masters of harmony,

The scientists of enthusiasm,

The flames that unite the fires of compassion and love;

For it is in the knowledge of ourselves that we are reborn free

Herein lies the secret of Eternity.

because i love you

The **Onionhead**® family holds ourselves responsible for the health and well being of all the world's children.

needs Save the Rain

In the developing world, a child dies every 15 seconds from lack of clean water. For these children, we have created our sister non profit called Save the Rain. We teach communities in Africa to build rain catchment systems as a sustainable water supply, using only local materials and local work force. Our budget is $15.00 for a child to have clean water for the rest of their life and the lives of their offspring. Visit www.savetherain.org

needs Onionhead®

In the way we believe the rain is the answer for the developing world, we believe the ability to handle our emotions intelligently is the answer for the developed world. Based on our concern for the environment, all of our products are printed on 100% recycled paper with non-toxic ink and made in the U.S.A.

...the beginning